Kept In Heart

For the moments, faces, and bonds that never fade

Magnollia Bandopadhyay

BookLeaf Publishing
India | USA | UK

Made with ❤ on the BookLeaf Publishing Platform
www.bookleafpub.in
www.bookleafpub.com

Dedication

To the ones who held my hand before I knew how to walk this world—
To the ones who smiled through my storms and laughed in my light—
To those who taught me how to love, fall, rise, and stay true—
This is for you.
For Papa, Mummy, Didi
For him, whose love turned silence into song
And **for the friends** who stood like poetry when words ran out.
You all are the ink in these pages, the heartbeat behind every verse.

Preface

This book is a map of my heart – a quiet collection of verses drawn from the *deepest corners of love, memory, and gratitude*. In these pages live the echoes of laughter, the warmth of embraces, and the lessons whispered in moments both gentle and fierce.

Every poem is a reflection, not only of who I am but of who shaped me. My parents, with their unwavering love and quiet sacrifices; my love, who awakened new colors in my world; and my friends, who stood by me like stars in my sky—each has left an imprint that turned into a line, a stanza, a story.

This collection is not perfect, nor polished with the world's expectations. **It is real, raw, and deeply mine.**

Acknowledgements

I owe every word in this book to the souls who made my life poetic.

To my parents—thank you for the values, the strength, and the quiet faith you planted in me. Your love is the foundation of every verse I write.

To the one who taught me how love feels when it is true —thank you for being both muse and memory.

To my friends, who listened, laughed, and lingered through my highs and lows—you reminded me that friendship is the purest kind of poem.

And lastly, to the *version of myself that kept writing through every emotion*—thank you for never letting go of your voice.

This is our shared story, in rhythm and rhyme.

1. A Poem for My Pillars

When morning breaks and silence sings,
My heart recalls its rooted wings.
The love that held me, soft yet strong—
A quiet truth I've known all along.

Let me speak of those who shaped my light.

Three souls who gave my roots their name—
My papa, mummy, and sister's flame.
They built my world, both strong and tall,
A steadfast love, the fiercest wall.
I stand today, through joy and strife,
Because they breathed into my life.
Not just a woman, but one who sees
The worth of grace and dignities.
They taught me how to walk with care,
To give, to listen, and to share.
To speak with heart, and think with grace,
And hold respect in every place.
How do I thank the hands that gave

A home, a truth, a love so brave?
Perhaps in words, though small they seem—
This poem is stitched from every dream.

2. The Man Behind my Wings

The youngest one, that's what I am,
Yet now I sing of a steadfast man.
The only one, our household's light—
My papa, strong and always right.
Since days my memories first began,
He was my friend, not just a man.
He'd tease and laugh, I'd scold and glare,
Even when I had but baby hair.
He raised me bold, with lion's will,
Yet held me soft, so calm and still.
He showed me how to stand and fight,
But called me princess every night.
If I would long for fruit in May,
He'd bring it home without delay.
The fridge would burst with mango's gold—
A quiet love, so brave and bold.
He doesn't know, but he's the flame
That shaped my soul, that gave me name.
His smile, a prize I'd chase for miles,

Just to bring back its shining smiles.
From him I learned to love with grace,
To hold my ground, to find my place.
My guide, my shelter through the test—
My papa, truly, is the best.
And as I stand with voice so clear,
I say with pride for all to hear:
My greatest gift, my life's own thread—
Is him, the man who gently led.

3. The Flame That Came from Her

She is my mother—soft yet strong,
Who carried me with love so long.
Nine months beneath her beating heart,
Where strength was stitched into my start.
They say a mother tends and feeds,
She hums the songs, she meets the needs—
But mine did more than tales reveal,
Her courage forged my soul of steel.
The first to rise when dawn was dim,
The last to sleep when night grew grim.
She cooked, she cleaned, with gentle grace,
Yet wore resolve upon her face.
Through every chore and every care,
She taught of life—how none play fair.
"Some lift you up, some drag you low,
But stand your ground and let them know."
Her stories, once dismissed as mild,
Now echo truths I've reconciled.
The fables spun by lantern light

Prepared me for the world's rough fight.
A teacher not by trade, but soul,
She shaped my thoughts, she made me whole.
A beacon in my darkest hour,
She gave me roots, and gave me power.
My mother, mum, or mummy dear,
The bravest voice I'll ever hear.
From her, I learned to chase the flame,
To walk through fire and still remain.
She placed the spark within my chest,
To speak my truth, to give my best.
A lioness in quiet form—
Who raised a storm within the storm.

4. My Second Mother

She came not as a mother, yet played the part,
With gentle hands and a delicate heart.
A sister first, yet more she became,
A friend, a guide, a sacred flame.
She wore each role with quiet grace,
A tender smile upon her face.
She danced through life with artful might,
And taught me dreams take rooted flight.
The brush, the thread, the dance, the song—
She led me there, where I belong.
She taught me how a home stands tall,
With love that weaves through rise and fall.
When words were new upon my tongue,
She sang the truths that must be sung.
Of father's toil, in silent hours,
Of mother's strength through storm and showers.
She whispered soft of loving me,
Of what it means just to be free.
She showed me what it means to share
A sister's bond beyond compare.

We laughed through nights with music loud,
Sang off-key and danced so proud.
Did makeup, fought with pillow blows,
Then made up quick—as true love knows.
Though years would cast her as the guide,
Now I, grown strong, walk by her side.
Yet still she shines, my northern star,
Who taught me love is who we are.
Time weaves us close through change and tide,
A bond no wind can break or hide.
For roots run deep where hearts have grown,
And in her light, I've always known.

5. The Quiet Shape of Love

What is this thing we speak of—Love?
A word oft tossed, both low and high above.
Some say it's duty, others say delight,
But none have nailed it clean and right.
Now lend an ear, both young and old,
Before you let your stories unfold.
If you claim love and call it true,
Here are a few things love must do:
Love is like friendship in full bloom—
With laughter dancing through the room.
It leans on trust and comfort shared,
Like trees that grow because they cared.
It's thinking not of self, but they—
Their hunger first at end of day.
It's not a chain, nor bond of fire,
But gives you wings to lift you higher.
It's home—the hearth, the worn-out chair,
Where peace and warmth hang in the air.
It's quiet strength, not loud control,
It gives you space, and keeps you whole.

It's honoring paths not quite your own,
And letting others stand alone.
Not sacrifice with heavy sighs,
But care that sees through others' eyes.
It takes a stand when things go wrong,
Yet mends with love, and makes you strong.
It's pulling close, then letting go,
To help each other rise and grow.
Love is teamwork, plain and fair,
No single heart can do its share.
But side by side, the work turns sweet—
Two steady hands, one rhythmic beat.
It sees the needs you do not speak,
The tears you hide, the days you're weak.
From custom, thought, or quiet pain,
It learns to listen like the rain.
And if you wonder how I love—
Just turn the page; there's more thereof.

6. When Eyes First Spoke

I still recall that fated day,
A room of faces in bright array.
To them, a stranger passing through,
To me, eight souls I somehow knew.
The little ones beamed with gentle grace,
While peers dismissed my quiet face.
Some sought favor with practiced charm,
Yet none could stir my heart alarm.
Then there he stood with fleeting eyes,
Catching my glance in shy disguise.
As I prepared my words with care,
He watched me speak from over there.
The topic spun my thoughts in flight,
Yet he remained within my sight.
Our gazes met – a silent start,
A smile exchanged, and so – my heart.
From that small spark, a thread was spun,
A tale begun, and now it's one.
What once was chance, now feels divine,
A moment born – and now he's mine

7. When Dreams Found a Face

The man of my dreams never had a face,
A shadowed figure time couldn't trace.
He came from behind, in dreams so deep,
To guard my heart while I lay in sleep.
He brought with him the breeze and light,
And butterflies in silent flight.
Each dream he entered soft and bright,
Yet stayed unknown, beyond my sight.
In slumber's tales, I saw a fight—
My knight emerged, bathed in white light.
Through storms he rode, through flame and dust,
To lift me high with strength and trust.
He'd kiss my brow with hands so kind,
A gentle peace I'd rarely find.
So tall he stood in dreamland's grace,
I knew he'd have a handsome face.
Then came the day I saw him near,
His gaze unsure, but full of cheer.
His eyes, they danced when meeting mine,

And spoke of truths he couldn't define.
He stumbled words, yet dropped his clues,
In riddles soft, he shared his views.
Too shy to say what bloomed inside,
But love, once sown, no heart can hide.
And on a wind-swept, golden day,
The butterflies returned my way.
He wasn't close, yet felt so near—
His voice came warm and pure and clear.
Not three small words, but something new:
"The girl I mentioned—it's you."
And just like that, the dreams made sense—
A tale of fate and no pretense.
A face took shape where none had been,
A truth unveiled from deep within.
And there he stood, both bold and true—
The man of my dreams, did have a face.

8. Rain lit Promises

It rained that day—the skies turned grey,
Yet nature smiled to bless our way.
We clasped our hands beneath the skies,
Our first soft touch, so shy, so wise.
A love so pure, so still, so deep,
Like quiet woods where secrets sleep.
No need for words, no grand display,
Just hearts that leaned and chose to stay.
I wrote to him everyday, late at night,
Each message lit his screen with light.
I'd borrow coins from mom's old phone,
To send him love when I was alone.
My codes were simple, soft, and few,
Each "good night" held a world so true.
His balance low, he could not write,
But missed calls echoed pure delight.
No soul around could ever guess
The quiet bond we did possess.
A vow we made, without a sound,
To hold each other, safe and bound.

Through joy and storm, in peace or pain,
In falling leaves and growing grain,
Not just in life, but evermore—
For seven lives and maybe more.

9. The Serpent in the Garden

I can't restrain the stirrings of my heart,
For aye, I love him—deep and bold and true.
He plays the jester and yet wounds with art,
He vexes me, yet paints my spirit new.
So whole I feel within his soft embrace,
My soul hath found its rest, its dwelling-place.
His smallest deed, his glance, his hurried pace,
Brings joy unmeasured time cannot erase.
He steals my portrait with a silent eye,
Then hands me water when my throat runs dry.
Though youngest in my kin, with much to bear,
'Twas in his smile I shed my daily care.
Yet purity oft draws the foul and vile,
And joy must walk through shadows for a while.
No plague nor fever struck our bond with dread—
But wicked hearts by envy's poison led.
A serpent slithered near our sacred flame,
And cast upon our love a cruel shame.
With cunning words and webs of dark deceit,
It sought to drag us down in sly defeat.

And lo, the bond that heaven's hand had tied,
Was bruised by malice, yet not cast aside.

10. When Heart Defy the Winds

We fought for love beneath the skies,
While clouds would gather, cold and wise.
Though tempests sought to pull apart,
We held the tether, heart to heart.
Among the hills where silence lay,
We met the trials of each day.
Though whispers stirred in passing air,
We found our peace in quiet care.
The world would speak in doubtful tone,
And plant its seeds where none had sown:
"Can such a bond as this abide?"
"Will time not wear what hearts confide?"
"Art thou two souls too much askew?"
"Can love like thine be truly true?"
But we, like trees by river fed,
Let not their words disturb our stead.
(A voice, soft as breeze among the leaves)
O meddling world, why ask again,
If joy must suffer to be plain?

Let not another tale be cast,
Where love like Juliet's cannot last.
For we had storms and nights of rain,
Yet each would bring us close again.
If one grew weary, lost in fear,
The other stood with presence near.
He'd touch my hand with quiet grace,
Or light a smile upon his face.
No gold, no vow, no crown, no pride—
Just truth that walked the lane beside.
They tried to bend what we had grown,
But roots run deep when love is sown.
Though many winds their trials threw,
We bloomed once more, and stronger too.

11. Bound by Divine Promise

This love, so pure and true,
No hands could break, no words could undo.
Through troubled paths, we walked our way,
Yet faith knew there'd come a brighter day.
The trials came, both fierce and wide,
I tried to bear, I tried to hide.
But deep within, my heart would see,
That love like this was meant to be.
Though struggles rose and hopes were thin,
God's plan was etched in me, within.
To walk with him, to share a life,
To be his love, to be his wife.
This love, so pure, is mine to keep,
A promise sown, a vow so deep.
For in this heart, I now believe,
What God had meant, I will receive.
With him, I'll live the dream we've spun,
A life of joy, beneath the sun.

To bear our children, strong and kind,
And be the happiest soul, entwined.

12. No Blood, Yet Bonded

As kin are praised and hearts unfold,
There's more to speak than bloodlines told.
For strangers once, now close to me—
They bloomed into my family.
No childhood bond, no schoolyard days,
No shared old lanes or playground haze.
But still, in halls of learning new,
Two souls appeared—so rare, so true.
The world was masked, the doors were shut,
Yet through the glass, our hearts stayed put.
No walls could block what fate had planned,
Three seeds took root in common sand.
From notes exchanged and sleepy calls,
To laughs that bounced through lecture halls.
Reminding one another when
Attendance struck its clock again.
From backs we had to backs we gave,
In silent strength, we each behaved.
No need for words when glances speak,
This bond we built is calm and deep.

Though storms may rage and voices roar,
Their presence heals me to the core.
A peace within the noise and strife—
They are the calm within my life.

13. Of Paper Balls and Golden Bonds

We called ourselves the Musketeer three,
A trio stitched in mischief and glee.
The thread of laughter, wild and bright,
Was spun in days and stitched just right.
What once began through screens and sound,
Grew firm when we met on solid ground.
While others scribbled notes with care,
We passed around our lunch to share.
When nerves ran high in viva's sway,
We tossed paper dreams and laughed away.
No fear could find its room to stay,
When friends like this lit up the day.
In every win I chanced to find,
Two voices echoed, soft and kind—
"Bravo to you! So proud, indeed!"
Their joy became my only need.
Though paths may part, as journeys do,
I send a silent prayer for you:
That blessings bloom where'er you go,

And smiles upon your faces glow.
So now I write, with simple pen,
To sing the worth of dearest friends.
For though these words are small and few,
They hold my heart, and all it knew.

14. The Bloom She Bought

I speak today of one so dear,
No blood we share, yet she feels near.
Not just a friend who comes and goes,
But one who stays through highs and lows.
She tends my wounds when days grow gray,
And lifts my heart in her own way.
She laughs with me at strangers' charm,
And shields my soul from silent harm.
The only one who gifts me blooms,
Without request, she fills my rooms.
She loves to hold the fleeting time,
In photos caught, in frames of rhyme.
We painted dreams with hues so wide,
An art begun, yet not supplied.
That canvas waits, though time has passed—
Two years have flown, but love will last.
She's far away, with dreams to chase,
Yet still I see her gentle face.
She builds her world with care and might,
And carves her path in morning light.

I miss her more than words can show,
Yet deep within, I always know—
She’s loved, she's strong, she walks her way,
And I just hope she shines each day.

15. A Friendship with No Filter

Here he comes, not just a friend,
But chatter's charm that knows no end.
A soul so warm, so strangely dear,
Who calms my doubts and calms my fear.
He never judged the way I'd be,
But let me breathe and set me free.
In every talk, in every jest,
He brings to life what I love best.
It matters not the miles we tread,
Or if each day our words are said.
For hearts like ours don't lose their tune—
We share the sun, we share the moon.
I still recall those early days,
When shy glances met in silent ways.
He'd judge a bit, I'd tease him more,
And laughter echoed from the floor.
From whispered jokes in classroom shade,
To bites of food we slyly made.
We grew in steps, from page to plan,

From reckless youth to teaching man.
Now reels are sent on hectic life,
On lessons taught and student strife.
Though we may not meet each morn,
Our bond is stitched and never torn.
And so I wish him joy and peace,
A heart that blooms and never cease.
May love soon knock upon his door—
A girl to tease forevermore.

16. Mischief in My Fingers

Now let me share a tale of me,
A glimpse into my history—
A girl who walked her winding lane,
Now nearing twenty-six, not plain.
It might seem like a tale you've heard,
With childhood chaos, wild and stirred.
Back to the days of teeth like pearls,
I ruled my world in frilly twirls.
At barely two, I made some noise,
Not with my toys—but bolder joys.
Though letters I could not yet read,
I'd mimic symbols, match with speed.
One quiet day, no soul in sight,
I held the phone with sheer delight.
A number pulled from leaflet print—
A jewelry shop, a playful stint.
I dialed and babbled, day by day,
Not knowing what my words would say.
To strangers kind, I'd coo and hum,
And find it fun, not knowing what'd come.

But one day came a call anew,
They asked, "May we speak with someone true?"
A voice replied, with calm and care,
"There's been a trace—we're getting there."
They tracked our home, that cheeky feat,
While I just smiled, so small and sweet.
"Police are coming, Mom!" I said—
"Let's meet and play!"—no hint of dread.
She asked me how it came to be,
I told her all, quite cheerfully.
No scoldings came, no sirens loud,
Just chuckles soft beneath a cloud.
And from that day, a rule was sworn—
The keypad locked, the cord was torn.
No more calls from tiny hands,
No secret chats or bold demands.

17. Whispers of my Younger Days

I speak of teens, those restless years,
So full of laughter, dreams, and tears.
When books and bells rang through the halls,
Yet playgrounds held my heart in thralls.
While girls would gather, soft and sweet,
To sit and talk or rest their feet,
I chased the sun with boys at play,
And wished the games would never stray.
Recess was gold, my shining prize,
And every class, a plan to devise—
To fake a cough or act unwell,
Just for a while to break the spell.
You'd find me out beneath the sky,
With younger kids who'd run and try—
The elders too, they knew my name,
We played as one, no need for fame.
But truth be told, I had my grace
In crafts and songs and every place.
An all-rounder, they called me so,

In every show, I'd brightly glow.
My Bengali folks with pride would teach
The arts of rhythm, heart, and speech.
And while they danced and painted dreams,
I wove my love in movie scenes.
SRK's charm and Shahid's gaze,
Set love alight in dreamy haze.
So if I seek a love that's grand,
It's cinema that shaped my stand.
Thus passed my early teens, you see,
In joy, in play, in reverie.
With books in hand and stars in sight,
I grew with wonder, bold and bright.

18. The Last Lessons of the Carefree Days

Then came the days of older teens,
When love slipped softly through the scenes.
And truth be told, in every heart,
A crush will form, a fleeting spark—
Be it a teacher, senior's gaze,
Or stars we watched through dreamy haze.
And just like that, school met its end,
But college came, with laughs to lend.
With friends half wild, yet true and dear,
We made some bonds that still stay near.
Between the lectures, stress, and tests,
We carved out joy, and found our best.
On campus corners, green and wide,
Where music played and thoughts would glide.
From benches bright where stories grew,
To libraries hushed, with words we knew.
The professors saw the spark in me,
Their praise still feels like melody.
They gave me more than just a grade—

A kind of love that doesn't fade.
As kids we'd dream, with eyes so wide,
Of grown-up days with adult pride.
We'd watch our elders come and go,
Earning their means, with steady flow.
But now I see what they had said—
To hold youth close before it's fled.
For once you start the workday race,
The world becomes a faster place.
Oh how I wish to turn the page,
To younger days, a softer stage.
To school, or halls of college bright,
Where laughter echoed pure delight.

19. Where I Once Sat

Now I'm a teacher, lighting minds anew,
But once I sat in the student's view.
Their curious eyes, so bright and wide,
Remind me of the past I hide.

In school, I walked the silent rows,
A studious soul, as learning goes.
In college halls and lecture days,
I earned my path through steady ways.

But joy was mine in lighter things—
In whispered laughs and secret flings.
I loved the chatter, soft and sly,
That drifted through the hallways high.

With books in hand, I'd make my way
To staffroom doors in hopes they'd say
A thing or two with careless cheer—
Some grown-up talk for me to hear.

Their lunchbox tales, their shopping plans,
The way they spoke with waving hands.
We'd guess which hearts were shyly tied,
And whisper names we thought had lied.

Yet more than that, I loved them well—
A love too deep for words to tell.
On Teacher's Day, my gifts were made,
With care and color gently laid.

At New Year's too, a card would go,
To thank them more than they might know.
They were the stars that lit my skies,
Who taught me truth and made me rise.

And some, with quiet grace and might,
Had sparked in me this guiding light.
They showed me how a soul could grow—
By giving all to help it glow.

And now I see, through time and grace,
The path that brought me to this place.
What once was theirs, now lies with me—
To guide, to love, to help them see.

20. Before the Real World Knocks

So here within these lines I write,
A glimpse of life in morning light.
A tale of where I stand today,
And thoughts I'd like to pass your way.

To those who've not yet turned twenty-five,
Whose youthful hearts are yet to strive—
Life as a child is wild and free,
With dreams as vast as sky and sea.

You sleep with peace, you play with glee,
No weight of stress or destiny.
You tear through days without a care,
And find delight most anywhere.

Oh, school—the golden, gleaming phase,
Of silly games and sunlit days.
You love some teachers, some you don't,
You call them names, though know you won't.

You share your tiffin, swap your books,
Exchange sly grins and knowing looks.
You plot to skip the dullest class,
By saying, "Ma'am, we need to pass—
To fetch the water, help our friend,"
The oldest trick that doesn't end.

You learn a bit, but more you see,
A glimpse of what the world might be.
You see how kind and cruel it spins,
And where a stranger's mask begins.

But college—ah! It shifts the frame,
And life no longer feels the same.
You taste the breath of being free,
Yet choices weigh quite heavily.

You choose your path, your voice, your name,
And not all days are bright with flame.
Yet hardship hides from you, just still,
You're dancing on a youthful hill.

Some graduate and start their climb,
Into the grown-up world of time.
While others seek a longer stay,
In books and dreams for two more Mays.

But oh! The life we once admired,
The job, the suit, the role desired—
Now feels more tight than we had guessed,
With silent weights upon your chest.

So hear me now, dear youth so bright,
Live fully in your present light.
For once you cross that unseen gate,
The world may trade your joy for fate.

Enjoy the dawn, the noon, the play,
Before the night steals youth away.
Hold close each laugh, each reckless run,
Before the grown-up race's begun.

21. The Final Verse

And now we come to the final page,
The last of twenty-one in stage.
No lofty words, no lessons grand—
Just a gentle close, just where I stand.

Life, as I know it, feels just right,
With all my loved ones held in sight.
But here I pause, in quiet grace,
To name a few who found their place.

For life as a teacher, I have learned,
Is more than just the knowledge earned.
It thrives when two things both align—
Their marks must rise, their eyes must shine.

When my students, bright with pride,
Speak my name with love inside—
That joy is one no words can weigh,
It lights my soul in its own way.

And I have seen these dreams come true,
In tender hearts, in scores that grew.
It humbles me, it lifts me high—
To know I've touched a life, a why.

So here I end, not with goodbye,
But thanks to those who stood nearby.
To God, to time, to love I've known—
This book of mine, is not mine alone.

22. A Thank you Note to You, Dear Reader

As these pages come to rest,
I offer you not an end, but a breath—
A pause before the next begins,
Where deeper truths and tales still spin.

For this is but a gentle start,
A glimpse into my world, my heart.
Someday—sooner or later, you'll see—
A next part will come, more raw, more free.

There are stories still that wait their turn,
Emotions yet to rise and burn.
And when the time feels right and true,
I'll place them in these pages too.

Till then, thank you—for every glance,
For walking with me through each chance.
This book is mine, yet now it's yours—
A shared reflection, gently poured.